The Truth Behind
History's Spookiest Spirits

by Rebecca Felix

Raintree is an imprint of Capstone Global Library Limited, a company incorporated in England and Wales having its registered office at 264 Banbury Road, Oxford, OX2 7DY – Registered company number: 6695582

www.raintree.co.uk
myorders@raintree.co.uk

Edited by Aaron Sautter
Designed by Bobbie Nuytten
Picture research by Gina Kammer
Production by Laura Manthe
Printed and bound in China.

ISBN 978 1 4747 0449 6 (hardcover)   ISBN 978 1 4747 0454 0 (paperback)
19 18 17 16 15   20 19 18 17 16
10 9 8 7 6 5 4 3 2 1   10 9 8 7 6 5 4 3 2 1

British Library Cataloguing in Publication Data
A full catalogue record for this book is available from the British Library.

Acknowledgements
Bridgeman Images: Archives Charmet/Bibliotheque des Arts Decoratifs, Paris, France/Adoration scene at the ancestral altar (w/c on paper), Chinese School, (19th century), 9, Archives Charmet/Bibliotheque Nationale, Paris, France/Spiritistic seance, from 'Fotografie di Fantasmi' by E. Imoda, 1912, French Photographer, (20th century), 19, Stavropol Museum of Fine Arts, Stavropol, Russia/Ivan IV (1530-84) the Terrible Visited by the Ghosts of Those He Murdered (pen & ink with bodycolour on paper), Klodt von Jurgensburg, Baron Mikhail Petrovich (1835-1914), 14; Getty Images: cass greene, 21, Hulton Archive, 20, 23, Lluis Real, 28, Print Collector, 12, 25; Mary Evans Picture Library, 18, 22; Newscom: Album/AMBLIN/UNIVERSAL, 26, SUN, 27, WARNER BROTHERS/GEFFEN FILM, 29; Shutterstock: Bill McKelvie, 13, Dan Kosmayer, 8, Eric Isselee, 17, GraphicStore, (calligraphic design) cover, Jiri Vaclavek, 16, katalinks, 15, KUCO, 7, llaszlo, (background) cover, 1, Marek Stefunko, 10, Pecold, 11, Slava Gerj, cover, 1, Thanapun, 4, Unholy Vault Designs, 24; Wikimedia: BrownieCharles99, 5

Design Elements
Shutterstock: Ensuper (grunge background), Larysa Ray (grunge frames), Slava Gerj (grunge scratched background)

We would like to thank David Gilmore, Professor of Anthropology at Stony Brook University, New York, for his invaluable help in the preparation of this book.

Contents

A terrifying encounter

In the middle of the night, a man and woman wake up with an eerie feeling. They look out of their bedroom window and see two eyes staring back from the darkness. Suddenly they hear their children screaming. They race to the children's room to find the beds banging up and down on the floor. Clothes, toys and books are flying through the air. The terrified parents grab their children and flee from the house. Some people think that spooky encounters such as this could be caused by only one thing – ghosts!

WHAT ARE GHOSTS?

Ghosts are said to be the **souls** of people who have died. They're usually invisible or **translucent**, and are often shaped like a person. Some people believe that ghosts are proof of an **afterlife**. Losing a family member or close friend can be hard for people to accept. Believing that their spirits live on after death can be very comforting.

Ghosts in ancient stories and modern tales aren't always friendly, however. Throughout history, ghost stories have often described spirits that enjoy terrifying the living. In several tales, ghosts seek revenge for wrongs committed against them in life. Whatever their motives are, these spooky spirits have haunted people's imaginations for thousands of years.

soul the spiritual part of a person

translucent almost transparent, allowing some light to pass through

afterlife the life that begins when a person dies

In 1975, the Lutz family reported being terrified by angry spirits at this house in Amityville, New York, USA. Their story was later turned into a best-selling book and film.

CHAPTER 1
Ancient ghost beliefs

Beliefs about ghosts and spirits are found throughout history. Many ancient cultures followed specific customs for dealing with dead bodies. They wanted to be sure that the spirits of the dead were happy in the afterlife.

ANCIENT BURIAL BELIEFS

In ancient Egypt it was believed that people's spirits could return to their bodies after death. The Egyptians often **mummified** dead bodies to keep them whole. They believed that mummies provided homes for people's spirits to come and go as they pleased.

In ancient Greece it was believed that people's souls travelled to the **Underworld**. When people died their bodies were usually buried with food and money. The Greeks believed that the dead needed these supplies to reach the afterlife. Without them, the spirits of the dead were thought to remain in the world to haunt the living. Most ancient Greeks weren't scared of such spirits. But they didn't want to be haunted by them either! Burying bodies properly was very important in ancient Greece.

mummify to preserve a body with special salts and cloth to make it last for a very long time

Underworld place under the earth where ancient people believed the spirits of the dead went

FACT: The ancient Greeks believed the dead had specific uses for food and money after death. Food was given to the fierce three-headed dog Cerberus that guarded the entrance to the Underworld. Money was paid to the ferryman called Charon. He carried the dead across the river Styx so that they could reach the afterlife.

HONOURING ANCESTORS

Keeping the spirits of the dead happy was a goal in many cultures for hundreds of years. If angry ghosts haunted the living, people thought there could be scary and dangerous results. In many African cultures, people worshipped the spirits of dead family members. As long as people honoured their ancestors, they believed the spirits would give them good fortune. But if people disrespected the dead, the spirits might punish or even kill them.

KNOWN BY MANY NAMES

Long ago, the souls of people who returned from the dead were often called revenants. But ghosts have been known by many names through the years. Spirit, spook and spectre are general terms for all types of ghosts. A poltergeist is an invisible ghost that makes a lot of noise and likes to move or throw things. Apparitions are ghosts that can be seen. They're often human-shaped but are pale, transparent or glowing. A wraith is the appearance of a soul as it leaves a dying person's body. In certain ancient cultures, ghosts have also been called fairies, angels, ghouls or devils.

In ancient China people often made offerings of food and money to the spirits of their ancestors. It was believed that these offerings helped to provide for the needs of the dead during the afterlife.

FACT: In ancient China people sometimes took unusual steps to make the spirits happy. People often didn't want unmarried family members to be lonely after death. So they arranged "ghost marriages" for their dead loved ones.

CHAPTER 2
Haunted European history

A team of horses pulling a carriage races towards an old castle. As the horses draw near, it becomes clear that they have no heads. A headless coachman also bounces atop the carriage. Inside is a woman who does have her head – in her lap! It is England's Queen, Anne Boleyn, who was beheaded in 1536.

The ghost of a headless Anne Boleyn is just one of thousands of reported ghost sightings in England. Bloody **executions** often took place at castles across Europe. It was often thought that the spirits of the dead remained to haunt the places where they were killed.

Anne Boleyn and many others were killed at the Tower of London. Today, the Tower is said to be one of the most haunted places in the UK.

execution when a person is put to death as punishment for a crime

FACT: In the late 1600s, thousands of people across Europe were accused of being witches. Hundreds were found guilty and beheaded at Austria's Moosham Castle. Today the castle is said to be crawling with angry spirits!

EUROPEAN BELIEFS

As in ancient cultures, many people in Europe believed that souls lived on after death. They also thought that some people's spirits didn't move on to the afterlife. These spirits instead remained stuck somewhere between life and death.

The living were often terrified of such ghosts. They would scream, run away or even faint if they thought they saw one. Such reported hauntings and unexplained events frightened people across Europe for hundreds of years.

WHERE DID GHOSTS COME FROM?

People commonly believed that spirits remained in the world because of unfinished business. If someone was murdered, his or her ghost might haunt the killer to get revenge. Or if people were suddenly killed in accidents, their spirits might try to visit their families one last time. People also thought that some restless spirits were the result of improper burials.

It was also believed that a few ghosts had important duties to complete before they could move on. These ghosts were said to haunt the living to ask for their help. The spirits requested proper burials for their remains, or they asked people to help them complete their unfinished tasks. It was thought that helping spirits in this way allowed them to rest peacefully in the afterlife.

In William Shakespeare's play Hamlet, *the ghost of Hamlet's father asks him to seek revenge for his murder.*

In a few cases, ghosts were thought to appear to warn people of danger. For example, the ghost of the Green Lady is said to haunt Stirling Castle in Scotland. According to several reports, the ghost has appeared to people as an **omen** of house fires or similar disasters.

omen sign of something that will happen in the future

Stirling Castle, Scotland

WOUNDS AND WHISPERS

Many reported ghosts were believed to be murder victims. Because of their violent deaths, these spirits often appeared to have gruesome wounds. Some ghosts were even said to still have the murder weapons sticking out of their see-through flesh!

Ghosts were often said to float in the air like glowing wisps of smoke or mist. But invisible ghosts may have been the most frightening. People often reported feeling as if unseen eyes were staring at them. Sometimes they felt invisible fingers pinch them. There were also many reports of strange laughter or whispers from unseen sources.

In several old tales, murderers are haunted by the gruesome ghosts of their victims.

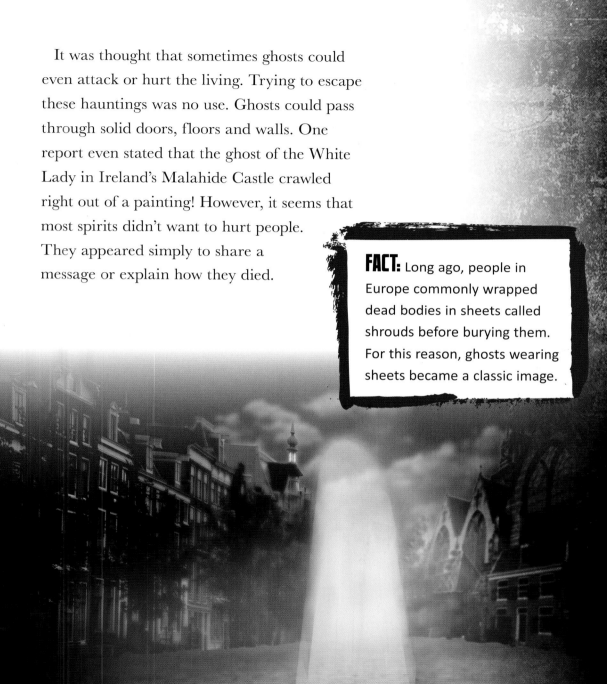

It was thought that sometimes ghosts could even attack or hurt the living. Trying to escape these hauntings was no use. Ghosts could pass through solid doors, floors and walls. One report even stated that the ghost of the White Lady in Ireland's Malahide Castle crawled right out of a painting! However, it seems that most spirits didn't want to hurt people. They appeared simply to share a message or explain how they died.

FACT: Long ago, people in Europe commonly wrapped dead bodies in sheets called shrouds before burying them. For this reason, ghosts wearing sheets became a classic image.

GETTING RID OF GHOSTS

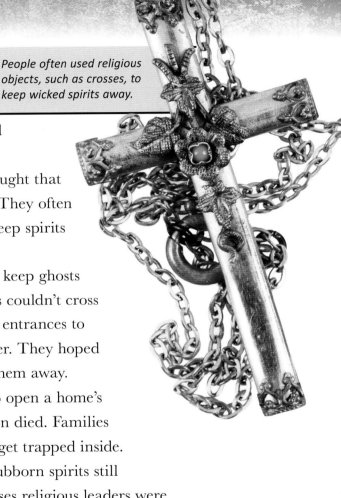

People often used religious objects, such as crosses, to keep wicked spirits away.

People across Europe developed several new beliefs and customs to prevent ghosts from haunting them. Many people thought that iron could harm or repel ghosts. They often pushed iron rods into graves to keep spirits from rising.

Some people wore **amulets** to keep ghosts away. Others believed that ghosts couldn't cross running water. They painted the entrances to their homes blue to look like water. They hoped this would fool ghosts and keep them away.

In England it was customary to open a home's doors and windows when a person died. Families didn't want the person's spirit to get trapped inside. But sometimes people thought stubborn spirits still haunted their homes. In these cases religious leaders were called in to perform **exorcisms** to force the spirits out.

FACT: Animals are reported as ghosts, too. The ghost of a large, black dog is said to haunt Leeds Castle. In Ireland the ghost of the angry Black Cat of Killakee is a popular legend. Both of these ghostly animals are said to be omens of death.

People's beliefs about ghosts and the supernatural lasted a long time. But by the 1700s people began learning more about science. Many became **sceptics**. They decided ghosts weren't real and that ghost sightings were made up. Strange events in the late 1800s, however, would soon change ghost history forever.

amulet small charm believed to protect the wearer from harm

exorcism religious ceremony performed to get rid of a spirit

sceptic person who questions things that other people believe in

CHAPTER 3
The rise of Spiritualism

As you lay in bed you suddenly hear loud rapping noises. Your heart beats faster as the noises grow louder. Should you run?

Margaret and Kate Fox didn't! In 1848, in New York, USA, these sisters instead chose to communicate with the ghost in their home. They bravely asked the spirit questions, not knowing how it would respond. The Fox sisters claimed that the ghost rapped out answers in codes to prove it was listening. With the help of their older sister, Leah, the sisters soon began holding sittings in their home. They wanted others to experience the ghost, too.

the Fox sisters, from left to right: Margaret, Kate and Leah

During ghost sittings in the 1800s, people often sat in a dimly lit room and held hands while trying to contact the spirits.

A NEW TREND

When news of the Fox sisters' ghostly encounters spread across the country, people were excited. Many were inspired to try communicating with the dead themselves. Seeking contact with ghosts soon became a major trend. By the late 1800s, interest in the supernatural spread and began a new movement called **Spiritualism**.

Spiritualism religion based on the belief that people can speak to the spirits of the dead

SPIRITUALISM AND SEANCES

During the late 1800s and early 1900s, Spiritualism spread like wildfire across the United States and Europe. **Seances** became very popular. Rather than running away from spirits, people invited them to show themselves. During a seance everyone kept silent as a **medium** called out to the dead. The table might then begin to shake as a ghostly voice was heard in the shadows. Sometimes invisible spirits seemed to spell out messages on "talking boards". Some mediums even claimed that ghostly forms appeared in **ectoplasm** that leaked from their skin, mouth or nose!

seance meeting to contact the spirits of the dead

medium person who claims to make contact with ghosts

ectoplasm slimy substance said to be produced by spirits during seances; it supposedly flows from a medium's body during a trance

During seances people were often startled when tables seemed to move or float into the air on their own.

The rise of Spiritualism and seances came along at a perfect time. Communication between people was changing. The telephone had recently been invented, which allowed people to hear the voices of others far away. People were also travelling faster than ever on railways and steamships. Time and distance seemed to be shrinking greatly in real life. Suddenly the idea of communicating with the dead in the afterlife didn't seem so impossible.

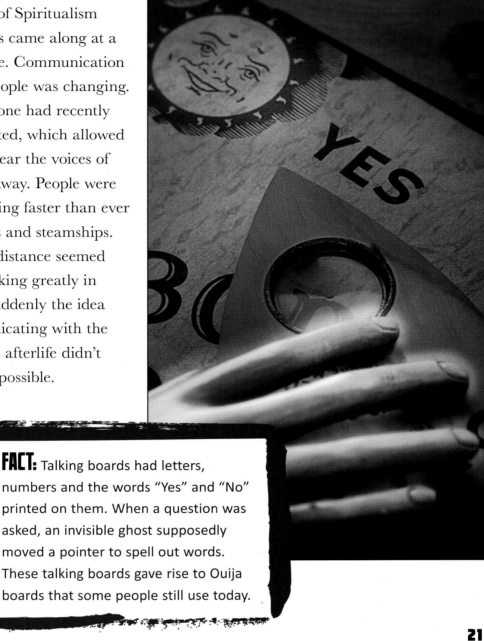

FACT: Talking boards had letters, numbers and the words "Yes" and "No" printed on them. When a question was asked, an invisible ghost supposedly moved a pointer to spell out words. These talking boards gave rise to Ouija boards that some people still use today.

SEANCE SCANDALS AND SCIENCE

Although Spiritualism became very popular, not everyone was swept up in the movement. By the late 1800s, many sceptics were working to prove that mediums were fakes, including the Fox sisters. They also looked for ways to prove whether or not ghosts were real. Organizations such as the Society of Psychical Research hunted for factual evidence of ghosts.

These organizations began using new technology to investigate reports of the supernatural. Soon, enough scientific evidence was found to prove that most mediums were fakes. Sceptics were able to show how mediums tricked people during seances. By the 1920s people began taking a greater interest in science, and Spiritualism began to fade away. But stories about ghosts continued to fascinate people everywhere.

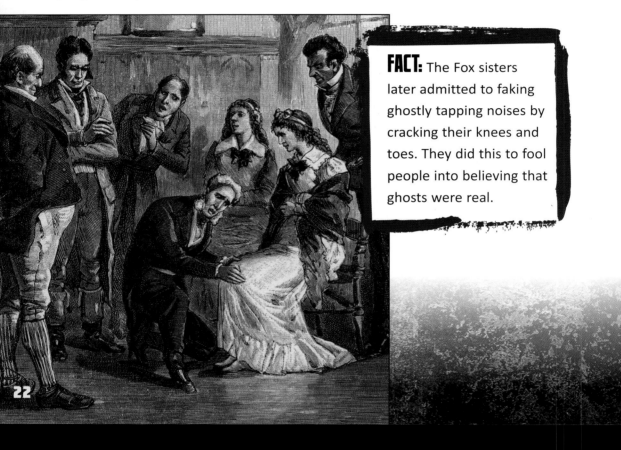

FACT: The Fox sisters later admitted to faking ghostly tapping noises by cracking their knees and toes. They did this to fool people into believing that ghosts were real.

22

Sceptics spent a lot of time investigating mediums and their fake activities at seances. They learned about an electrical device that some mediums hid in their shoes. A thread ran through the medium's clothing and was hidden in a sleeve. The medium simply pulled the thread to turn on the device, which made tapping noises under the table.

The dim lighting at seances also helped to cover up the mediums' tricks. For example, the guests couldn't see that mediums used their knees or hidden wires to lift or shake tables.

Mediums also used mixtures of soap, egg whites or toothpaste to make fake ectoplasm. They often swallowed this fake goo and spat it back up during a seance. People couldn't tell that the goo was fake in the dim lighting.

medium Marthe Beraud with fake ectoplasm coming from her mouth in 1910

CHAPTER 4
Haunting entertainment

Late one night, a schoolteacher rides his horse through a dark wooded area. His heart starts thumping as he thinks of the nameless terror that is said to lurk in this place. He knows the local tales about an angry, headless spirit that attacks intruders in the woods. Before long, the teacher's fears become real when a dark shape appears. It's another rider on horseback – but it's not human! It has no head and holds a large axe in its hand. The chase is on, but the teacher is doomed.

FICTIONAL LEGENDS

In the late 1700s and 1800s stories about spooky encounters with ghosts became very popular. These scary ghost stories were often told at parties and written about in newspapers, magazines and books. For example, the creepy tale of the headless horseman had been told for many years. In 1820, author Washington Irving wrote his own version of the story. His story, The Legend of Sleepy Hollow, quickly caught the public's imagination. This legendary tale has been a popular story ever since.

In many stories from the 1800s, ghosts often weren't given much to do. They usually just appeared, stared at people, and looked scary. In Charles Dickens' famous novel *A Christmas Carol*, however, ghosts are treated differently. Several spirits in this story show a miserable old man how to change his ways and live a better life. Dickens' story became a classic and is still popular to this day. It also influenced many future stories about ghosts.

The ghost of Jacob Marley is the first spirit to visit Ebenezer Scrooge in Charles Dickens' book A Christmas Carol.

TODAY'S POPULAR GHOSTS

In the 1900s, ghosts were as popular as ever, but people began thinking of them differently. Various spirits appeared in many popular books, films and cartoons. Most were still scary, but a few were friendly. *Casper the Friendly Ghost* was a cartoon created in the late 1930s. Casper was a lonely ghost of a boy who didn't want to scare anyone. Instead he was helpful and cheerful. He tried to be friends with the living.

In the 1980s ghosts became a source of humour in several stories. The 1984 film *Ghostbusters* features a green ghost called Slimer that eats a lot of food. He doesn't hurt anyone. But when he's cornered, Slimer sprays people with slimy green goo to get away. The main character of the 1988 film *Beetlejuice* is more like a clown than a ghost. He has supernatural powers, but enjoys playing pranks on people rather than hurting them.

In the 1995 film Casper, *the ghost becomes friends with a girl whose mother has died.*

Since the 1990s many stories have again featured ghosts as terrifying spirits. These ghosts are often wicked and enjoy scaring and killing people. Sometimes they meow like creepy cats or crawl on ceilings like spiders. They may even spin their heads all the way around!

FACT: Modern ghost hunting fascinates many people. Several TV programmes, such as the US programme *Ghost Hunters,* feature investigators as they look for spirits. They use special cameras and audio equipment to look for evidence of ghosts.

GHOSTS OF THE FUTURE?

Tales of ghosts have fascinated people for thousands of years. In recent years people have become much more sceptical about the existence of ghosts. But some people feel that ghost stories will always be popular. They say that many people will always believe their souls will live on after death. For this reason, people will probably always be interested in reported hauntings and ghost stories.

Today, writers and film-makers are creating new ways for ghosts to interact with people. Sometimes spirits even pop up inside people's TVs and computers. Who knows how ghosts might appear to people in the future? Perhaps they'll haunt us in ways we can't yet imagine!

NAME	APPEARANCES	STORY
Headless Horseman	old folktales; The Legend of Sleepy Hollow (1820)	A headless ghost chases victims on a horse and carries a large axe.
Ghosts of Christmas Past, Present and Yet to Come	*A Christmas Carol* (1843); several films based on the novel	Christmas spirits show a mean old man glimpses of his past, the present and his own future to teach him to change his ways.
Casper	1930s comics; *Casper* (1995)	The ghost of a friendly boy tries to be friends with humans and animals.
Slimer	*Ghostbusters* (1984)	A green, blob-shaped ghost covers people in slimy goo when cornered.
Beetlejuice	*Beetlejuice* (1988)	A wild and destructive spirit tries to help two ghosts scare humans away from their house.
The Voice	*Field of Dreams* (1989)	A ghostly voice guides a farmer to build a baseball field on his farm. Later, the farmer is reunited with the spirit of his dead father.
Sam Wheat	*Ghost* (1990)	The ghost of a man who is killed remains behind to solve his own murder and to protect the woman he loves.
Constance	*Monster House* (2006)	An angry spirit takes control of a creepy old house and terrorizes several children in the neighbourhood.

In the film Beetlejuice, *the title character is a mischievous spirit. He enjoys playing pranks on the living and causing chaos all around him.*

Glossary

afterlife life that begins when a person dies

amulet small charm believed to protect the wearer from harm

ectoplasm slimy substance said to be produced by spirits during seances; it supposedly flows from a medium's body during a trance

execution to put a person to death as punishment for a crime

exorcism religious ceremony done to get rid of a spirit

medium person who claims to make contact with ghosts

mummify to preserve a body with special salts and cloth to make it last for a very long time

omen sign of something that will happen in the future

seance meeting to contact the spirits of the dead

sceptic person who questions things that other people believe in

Spiritualism religion based on the belief that people can speak to the spirits of the dead

translucent almost transparent, allowing some light to pass through

Underworld place under the earth where ancient people believed the spirits of the dead went

Books

Ghosts and Other Specters (The Dark Side), Anita Ganeri (Wayland, 2010)

The Ghost Hunter's Guide (Monster Tracker), Charles Bouvier (Franklin Watts, 2011)

Ghosts and Haunted Houses (Solving Mysteries with Science), Jane Bingham (Raintree, 2013)

Websites

www.britannia.com/history/legend/borley.html
Learn all about the Borley Rectory, which is said to be the most haunted house in England.

www.gadling.com/2012/06/04/the-worlds-10-scariest-haunted-castles/
Discover and learn the history behind some of the most haunted castles in the world.

www.haunted-britain.com
Read about several spooky ghost stories and haunted castles across the United Kingdom.

Index